A Cup of Love

Without Racism, Love Rules the World

Dr. Janet L. Seay-Stanley

ROYSTON Publishing

BK Royston Publishing
P. O. Box 4321
Jeffersonville, IN 47131
502-802-5385
http://www.bkroystonpublishing.com
bkroystonpublishing@gmail.com

© Copyright – 2023

All Rights Reserved. No part of this book may be reproduced, stored in a retrieval system, or transmitted by any means without the written permission of the author.

Cover Design: Elite Cover Designs

ISBN-13: 978-1-959543-76-3

Library of Congress Control Number: 2023919517

King James Version Scriptural Text – Public Domain

The Message Bible - Copyright © 1993, 2002, 2018 by Eugene H. Peterson

New King James Version - Copyright © 1982 by Thomas Nelson. Used by permission. All rights reserved

Printed in the United States of America

ACKNOWLEDGEMENTS

To Jesus Christ, for friendship, input, and inspired advice.

A special thanks to my mama, Ms. Thelma Louise Horton, for her encouragement and for reading whatever I gave her to read.

To Pastor Vivian Snardon and Mrs. Anna Beason, for a wealth of knowledge about what life holds for us if we only tap into it.

To my daughters, Sharicka, LaTonya, and Yolanda, for constantly saying, "Mama, you can do it."

To both my late husbands, James E. Seay, Jr. and James T. Stanley, for pushing me toward perfection and listening to me beat myself up when it comes to writing. And, my new love, Jacob Northington, for being a special friend when I needed one after my second husband passed away.

To my friends and family for understanding my absence in the last thirteen years as I completed my education enough to write and bring forth *A Cup of Love* (2016).

TABLE OF CONTENTS

Acknowledgments	iii
Prologue	vii
Introduction - The "Will" to Choose	xi
Spiritual Recognition of Love to Forgive Ourselves	1
Spiritual Recognition of Love to Forgive Others	9
Praying From a Distance	13
We Did What?!!	17
Don't Diss Me! Words from a Disrespected Black Woman to Conceited Black Men	27
We Can Change Through Practices of Spiritual Discipline	33
The Reason We Love: We Are On a "Love" Mission – The author's theological research for God's love and what we as people are willing to change on our journey from here to heaven.	55
Questions for Personal Reflection or Group Discussion	81
Notes	85

Bibliography	87
About the Author	89

PROLOGUE

Don't Diss Me

(Words from A Disrespected Black woman)

"You Black men dare to diss me! After the slave masters whipped you, you not only needed my empathy but my warm breast to rest upon. Don't Diss Me!"

You Black men dare to diss me! After losing your job, you needed my ear to listen to your whining, and after giving you my ear, I gave you my money until you got back on your feet. Don't Diss Me!"

"You Black men dare to diss me! After my Christ died and you hid behind closed doors in fear for your lives, I tried to tell you that HE rose, but you called me crazy. He gave me the command to carry His resurrection message. If you don't believe me read Matthew, Mark, Luke, and John. Don't Diss Me!"

"You Black men dare to diss me! You called me senile and crazy because I'm rejoicing in Christ when He met me at Jacob's well. I thought you cared about me. Don't Diss Me!"

"You Black men dare to diss me! We carried you for nine months and nurtured you until you could develop into the patriarchal monster you are today. So, if I'm senile and crazy, you are the product of this senile and crazy African American woman. Don't Diss Me!"

"You Black men dare to diss me! You hid behind my educated mind when it came to talking to the insurance agent, the broker, the realtor, the Banker, the childcare director, the marriage counselor, the guidance counselor, and the judge. Remember, you wanted me to be silent. Don't Diss Me!"

"My fellow Black men, lend me your ears, I will not be silent! My Creator says to speak boldly and make it plain so that even you can understand. My Creator says that I am more than a conqueror, and I'm to be steadfast, unmovable, always abounding in the works of the Lord! So, you see, you don't have to diss me because we are one of the same bodies in Christ, who is the vine, and we are the branches. Christ is the body; you and I are the extremities. Christ is the Church in which we enter black with sin, and come out of the Church saved and as white as snow."

So, remember, if you diss me, you are dissing yourself. Don't Diss Me!

(Written on Sept. 1, 2006, at 9:00 am at Glencliff High School after reading *Not Without a Struggle,* by Bishop Vashti Murphy McKenzie).

INTRODUCTION

When we change into something more comfortable, it changes our mood. It's evening, the sun is going down behind the mountains, or if you are a southern girl like myself, it's going down behind the tall trees. It's only then that we humans get a sense of relaxing our thoughts from a day of thinking [too much] to a more comfortable and relaxed state. We want our minds relaxed along with our bodies.

Simply put, we just want to take off and put on something that will give us a sense of feeling safe, content, and serene because we feel we deserve this sereneness and relaxed state of mind, body, and soul. But all what I just stated is a metaphor to get to the real, ultimate deserved feeling of comfort within a body of love for self and others. To get to this point, we must practice a simple little thing— *love.*

The "Will" to Chose

To paraphrase the author of Leviticus 19:18, "We are to put off all malice, and put on brotherly love." How are we to do that so we can feel comfortable within ourselves? By recognizing first, the origin of love, the authenticator of love, the *cup* that holds the love, the God in us.

When we recognize, we are making ourselves aware, conscious of this ultimate love potion, "a cup of love." God is our cup of love which He has shown through the mercy given to Adam and Eve. He allowed them to live. Through the law, prophets, and the blood shed on the cross of His only begotten Son, Jesus the Christ, we live. To share "a cup of love," you must recognize the love in you first and foremost.

Interestingly, we ask ourselves daily, what is it that keeps us from recognizing the ultimate love we have inside to spread abroad? Interesting question; however, there is a dark evil spiritual presence here on earth with us that pulls at our conscious mind to hate, which is the opposite of love. And sometimes, we fall prey to this dark evil present state of mind by hating and disrespecting ourselves and others, which brings on malice [the intention or desire to do evil, ill will; law–wrongful–intention, especially as increasing the guilt of certain offenses]. This spiritual darkness is a story all by itself (laughing); we can fight it with "a cup of love."

In a letter, the book of Romans 7:11-19, the apostle Paul mentions the control of this darkness over the mind when he said, "For sin, taking occasion by the commandment, deceived me, and by it killed me. Therefore, the law is holy, and the command holy and just, and good. Has then what is good become death to me? Certainly not! But sin, that it might appear sin was producing death in me through what is good, so that sin through the commandment might become exceedingly sinful. For we know that the law is spiritual, but I am carnal, sold under sin. For what I am doing, I do not understand. For what I will to do, that I do not practice; but what I hate, that I do. If, then, I do what I will not to do, *(the mental faculty by which one deliberately chooses or decides upon a course of action he can finish the race if he wills it.)* I agree with the law that it is good. But now, it is no longer I who do it, but sin that dwells in me. For I know that in me *(that is, in my flesh)* nothing good dwells; for to will is present with me, but how to perform what is good I do not find. For the good that I will to do, I do not do; but the evil I will not to do, that I practice." NKJV 2013.

Spiritual Recognition of LOVE in Forgiving Ourselves

We must recognize the "cup of love" we have inside us that will help us love us and others. This recognition and practice of love is a remedy for malice, abuse, racial tension, and bullying (people and animals). Your "spiritual love light" shines brighter from inside to outside when you forgive yourself, first, for all past sins. Remember, God forgave you, so you must recognize that after you asked for forgiveness, it's over; there is NO more sin in you. Move on!

Other than the practices of discipleship that I will have at the end of my book, here are some suggestions on forgiving one's self,

1. **Practice self-acceptance**. You don't need forgiveness for being you. Forgiving yourself is about targeting the specific things that you feel bad about, not about the person you are. As a forgiveness technique, self-acceptance allows you to acknowledge that you're a

good person, faults and all. It doesn't mean that you ignore the faults or stop trying to improve yourself, but it does mean you value yourself above those elements and cease to allow your faults to halt your progression in life.

- Love yourself and give yourself permission to heal.
- Laugh more. It'll give you more freedom to stop taking it all so seriously.

2. **Understand the importance of forgiveness**. Living in a state of being unable to forgive requires a lot of energy. You are constantly chewed up by fear of your vulnerability, burning with anger with the source of pain, and living with the constancy of sadness, hurt, and blame. This energy deserves to be put to better use so that your creativity and abilities are fed, not your negativity. Forgiveness allows you to live in the present instead of the past, which means you can move into the future with a renewed sense of purpose focused

on change, improvement, and building on experience rather than being held back by past hurts.

- Some people are afraid to forgive themselves because they fear losing their sense of self that was built on the back of anger, resentment, and vulnerability. In this case, ask yourself if that angry, easily hurt, and reactive person is the identity you're keen to show the world and live with. Is the security of this mode of thinking worth the effort and harm it is causing you? It's better to have a small time of insecurity as you find your way again than to continue a lifetime bogged down in anger.
- See forgiveness in a positive light. If you're bothered that forgiving suggests you shouldn't experience strong feelings such as resentment and anger, try viewing it as the chance to feel strong positive feelings such as joy, generosity, and faith in yourself. Switching it to thinking about what you'll

gain rather than what you'll lose has the benefit of keeping you positive while minimizing negative emotions.

3. **Consider the challenges raised by not forgiving yourself.** Not only do you allow yourself to remain in the past, but not forgiving yourself takes a huge toll on your emotional and physical health. Inability to forgive is sourced from anger and resentment, two emotions that can wreak havoc with your health. Numerous studies have shown that people stuck in constant anger are more prone to disease and illness than people who can learn to forgive themselves and others.

- Always remember that forgiving doesn't equate with forgetting. You're entitled to learn by experience and be guided by the experience. It's about leaving aside the resentment and self-inflicted berating that comes with remembering.

4. **Think about what will improve in your life if you can release yourself and how to bring this to fruition.** As part of forgiving yourself, it's usually not enough to simply resolve to forgive yourself. Doing things to confirm the forgiveness process will help you realize your self-forgiveness and to give you a new sense of purpose. Some of the things you might like to consider doing include:

   - Taking up meditation. Meditation is an ideal way to find inner quiet, spiritual, self-realization, and physical relaxation. It will allow you to take time out, tune into and appreciate the moment, and get in touch with your inner self. Done regularly, meditation will improve your well-being and sense of self.
   - Affirm your self-worth. Remind yourself regularly that you are a valuable and beautiful person and say simply: "I forgive myself" or "I will no longer let

anger eat away at me," whenever the negative thoughts reappear.

- Keep a diary. Write down your journey to forgiveness. Having the writing space to share your thoughts and feelings with, one that nobody else will ever read, is a liberating and self-enlightening way to break through negative approaches to your life.
- If you have faith, draw strength from its teachings to support you.

5. **See forgiveness as a journey, not a destination**. If you're liable to think you're unable to "get to" self-forgiveness, you may be sabotaging your chances of even starting the forgiveness journey. It helps to accept that forgiveness is an ongoing process and you'll have your up days and your down days, as with most feelings and experiences in life. You may feel you have reached a point of forgiveness, only to have something happen

that causes you to feel it was all a wasted effort and you're back to square one, angry and annoyed with yourself. The best approach is to let the slip-ups happen and see them as minor setbacks in an otherwise more forgiving self.

- Learn what you've done in the past but value your whole self. Enjoy positive experiences consciously, and don't seek to downgrade them.
- Be grateful for what you do have–great relationships, a home, a family, an education, abilities, interests, hobbies, pets, health, etc. Look for the good in yourself.
- Be self-compassionate. Shift your thoughts to more fulfilling, value-focused things when negative reproaches arise.
  - Apologize if others have been involved and you have not already done so or you have not done so genuinely. Only do this when you have changed

your negative outlook and if doing so will not harm

that person.

Spiritual Recognition of LOVE in Forgiving Others

A Cup of Love can handle more than we can imagine. When you look at behavior from a spiritual perspective, the practices come easily. When we forgive ourselves, it becomes easy to forgive others. It was in "Hugs Daily Inspirations Words of Comfort" [a publication I received from my Social Work Department at Lipscomb University] that I realized that James 3:17 was directed at me. Real wisdom, God's wisdom, begins with a holy life and is characterized by getting along with others. It is gentle and reasonable, overflowing with mercy, and blessings.

Most of us find it difficult to forgive the people who have hurt us. And that's too bad because life would be much simpler and more pleasant if we could forgive people "once and for all" and be done with it. But forgiveness is seldom that easy. Usually, the decision to forgive is straightforward; it's the process of forgiving that's more difficult. Forgiveness is a journey that requires time, perseverance, and prayer.

If you sincerely wish to forgive someone, pray for that person – and keep praying. While you're at it, pray for yourself, too, asking God to heal your heart. Don't expect forgiveness to be easy or instantaneous, but rest assured that with God as your partner, you can forgive and enjoy a life of peace with those around you "Hugs Daily Inspirations Words of Comfort." Forgiving others is a journey we must go through to please the one who forgave while in agony, Jesus said, "Father, forgive them, for they know not what they are doing" (Luke 23:34, NIV).

I agree with the New York Times best-selling author Max Lucado when he said, "And when you think about it, they hadn't the faintest idea what they were doing.

They were a stir-crazy mob, mad at something they couldn't see, so they took it out on, of all people, God. But they didn't know what they were doing. Yes, the dialogue that Friday morning was bitter. The verbal stones were meant to sting. How Jesus, with a body racked with pain, eyes blinded by his own blood, and lungs yearning for air, could speak on behalf of some heartless thugs is beyond my comprehension. Never, never have I seen such love. If ever a person deserved a shot at revenge, Jesus did. But he didn't take it. Instead, he died for them. How could he do it? I don't know. But I do know that suddenly, my wounds seem very painless. My grudges and hard feelings are suddenly childish. Sometimes I wonder if we don't see Christ's love as much in the people he tolerated as in the pain he endured." (Max Lucado, On Calvary's Hill, 2013).

A Cup of Love, measured, pressed down, and given to those who hated him, why? Remember Romans 7, sometimes we listen to the darkness of our conscious mind. We will good to happen, but evil is always present, and therefore we must start practicing the spiritual disciplines of Christ, and forgiveness is just one of them. In his book, Bishop Jerry L. Maynard says it's a part of our maturing in Christ. He states, "After you have forgiven that person, you must take the next step and do as God did – 'Throw it into the depths of the sea' (Micah 7:19). In other words, don't bring it up again. Don't use that past deed as leverage to manipulate and attack that person in the future. When you see that person, you no longer get that gut-wrenching desire to give that person a piece of your mind. You no longer feel uncomfortable in their presence or hope for them to feel uncomfortable in yours" (Jerry L. Maynard, Bishop, Christian Maturity 2010).

Praying from a Distance: Focusing from Within

We must commune with God several times a day to get in the right relationship with the One who can transform our hearts and minds into that 'cup of love.'

From experience, I have learned that to be with God is comforting, and more so when He is with me. You'll learn to love yourself and others and forgive yourself and others. It comes easy now that I have a spiritually transformed heart that use to be lukewarm, not accepting the fact that God forgave me for all my past sins.

Constant prayer is a spiritual practice that transforms us. For example:

- Centering Prayer-To quiet the heart and rest in God alone.
- Contemplative Prayer-To develop an open, restful receptivity to the Trinity that enables me to always be with God just as I am.

- Conversational Prayer-To talk naturally and unselfconsciously to God in prayer times with others.
- Fixed-Hour Prayer-To stop my work and pray throughout the day.
- Breath Prayer-To pray a simple, intimate prayer of heartfelt desire before God.
- Inner-Healing Prayer-To assist the emotionally broken and wounded as they seek God for the healing only, he can give.
- Intercessory Prayer-To turn my concerns and worries into prayer; to enter God's heart for the world and then pray from there.
- Labyrinth Prayer-To make a quiet, listening pilgrimage to God.
- Liturgical Prayer-To open myself to God through established patterns or traditions of written prayers and readings.

- Fasting-To let go of an appetite to seek God on matters of deep concern for others, myself, and the world.

There's an old gospel song my friends and I use to sing as a group at Saint Peter A.M.E. Church back in Nashville, Tennessee. It goes like this: "The Jesus in me loves the Jesus in you; The Jesus in me loves the Jesus in you, so easy, so easy, so easy, so easy to love." Yes, love is applicable when you love and respect "you." When you do this, this is to look at "you" and question yourself, "Am I a pleasing person to be around others? If not, then why aren't I a pleasing person to be around others? Do I speak encouragement? Or, when others leave my presence, are they leaving with their heads low because of something I said? Evaluate yourself, you know when you are not loving yourself and others. Don't play games with yourself because God already knows you, He's just allowing you to see 'you.'

We Did What??

A Cup of Love is essential to have. The essence of this book is to prove to you what you already know, which is, there is love in you to share. So, take off the old you and put on the new you. All races, take off the old you and put on the new you. Example: Caucasian people, if you pull off the old you–your avoidance of seeing why you really came to America, and that is to get away from whence you came. The lack of food, bad water irrigation, crime, not wanting a Queen, but to be a Republic by-partisan nation. You were running away from the scene of child neglect and abuse (chimney sweepers). You were running away from something and found [you thought] was an empty land; you got happy and wanted to keep it for yourselves and not share it!

Caucasians, you killed off whoever stood in your way of "false" happiness. You became selfish; the life you wanted, the happiness you wanted all became "false" happiness. Your "cup of love" became a cup of hatred. There's a song we use to sing in elementary school by Woodie Guthrie, "This Land is Your Land." And I believed in that song so much that I would sing loud and clear, although I couldn't sing a lick, but I opened my mouth (in the Black-only school) and belted out… "This land is my land, this land is your land, from California, to the New York Islands. To the redwood forest to the Gulf Stream waters; this land was made for you and me."

America cannot be a land of the free until Caucasian people do some retrospection of the reason you came here and recognized that you listened to some bad apples in your own race.

Those type of bad apples will spoil the whole bunch. The practices of Christian disciplines will help you gain back your "cup of love" that's waiting to be used, and the "cup of love" will give you back the joy you once had when you saw this beautiful land. Yes, this land was waiting on you. God saw to it that it was seen by you, but it was also waiting for people not like you, with skin of a different color.

Caucasians, you sent out ads and flyers for workers, and you knew they were going to be a different color and race. When "they" came to help you fulfill your dream here, you allowed the bad apples, the Caucasians without a "cup of love" to mistreat and kill them. Them, the Chinese, the Japanese, the Asians, the Blacks, the Germans, the Irish, the Polish, the Mexicans, and the Cubans. In contrast to this awful image, Caucasians had already killed the Native Indians, the first inhibitors of this land you named "America."

When you see "yourself, then your "cup of love" inside will begin to see others as human beings and not objects. One of my favorite books is, "The Anatomy of Peace," by The Arbinger Institute. It tells how we must practice seeing each other as human beings and not objects.

I dare you to read this book. Like in childhood, we use to say, "I double dare you." God, our Creator, gave us a *free will*. We can *will* to be good or we can *will* to be evil; both have *end* rewards. You chose.

Nevertheless, in this book, my first book, I'm telling you to choose a "cup of love." And, Caucasians, stop shying away from finding out what another ethnic culture does during their stay here in America. You will never know about them when you shy away from them, hoping they will change and do things your way. Listen, if not "your way," it's "no way." On page 17 of my favorite book, "The Anatomy of Peace," the author talks about "recovering inner clarity and peace, getting out of the box." It lists three ways of getting out of the box you're in:

1. Look for the signs of the box (blame, justification, common box styles, etc.).
2. Find an out-of-the-box place (out-of-the-box relationships, memories, activities, places, etc.).

3. Ponder the situation anew (i.e., from this out-of-the-box perspective)."

The only difference between my book and their book is that they are asking you to get out of the box, and I'm asking you to get in the "cup of love" that you already have inside by putting yourself back into love, back into joy, and sharing it. The box and cup are just metaphors to begin your journey back to the love you once had and start respecting and loving yourself and others. Loving others is the key to joy and happiness. Stop listening to those who do not want joy and happiness; ignore them, and they will flee from you. This saying is a Scripture verse telling us to ignore Satan, a spiritually dark, evil entity, and he will flee and stop pestering us, because he realizes we're not turning back and playing his games of killing people because people do not look like you. Caucasians, trust the outcome of using your "cup of love" daily.

And, to my Black people, or whatever you want to call yourselves or whatever you want the Caucasians to call you, we came from a land rich in diamonds, gold, silver, and copper. Our lands were rich and green. We were family-oriented; we made do with what we had. We had joy making things like quilts, clothes, dishes, and weapons to kill animals for our dinner table. Our men mentored the boys, and when they came of age, they sent them out to fend for themselves, and "if" they came back after time in the jungle, it showed that they have become a man who could survive.

Our Black women nurtured girls (and boys), and showed them how to become young ladies and women. We were shipped and enslaved by other races from other lands. They used our strength as workers in their lands.

Black people, the Portuguese, France, Great Britain, Spain, and America used us to be servants for whatever reason, in whatever capacity. Black people, we suffered from the chains in the holding cages by the sea until ships came to merge us into one body; down below the belly of the ship. Black people, we continued to suffer at the hands of other races with illnesses our bodies were not used to. When the Portuguese, Spaniards, French, and British people came to their senses and recognized we were just as human as they were, they discontinued using and battering us and made laws not to hold us as slaves anymore.

    However, where they left off, America took up. Only now, we not only suffered from the chains of hatred, our women and men were hung, burned, and beaten. Also, since Caucasian males had a false sense of their penis not being able to satisfy their women, they figured that our black men would and they started castrating our men before lynching, during a lynching, and after the lynching. This false sense of penis length still haunts them today—false sense.

Nevertheless, regardless of how bad it was for the Black people in America during slavery, it does not even compare to what Black people are doing to each other now after becoming completely free to do whatever it takes to live by holding jobs, attending college, any anything to stay off the streets. Instead of recognizing the love we once had for our family, we destroy the family.

I see Black people killing Black people and making our race become "extinct." Not all Blacks fall into this category, we can say, "it's psychological." But it's more so spiritually induced. Remember, I paraphrased Lev. 19:18, "We are to put off all malice, and put on brotherly love." If we want to feel comfortable within ourselves, we should share this love and comfort with others.

Black people are stopping other Black people from living a well-deserved life of education, making it in the athletic world and the corporate field as business owners. Black people shoot down each other while achieving dreams. Why? I'm glad you asked me. Because if I do not have, you should not have either; malice. Black lives do matter, so stop killing each other. Recognize that you can love each other and return to the joy you once had toward each other.

Black people, you are good at finding and placing blame because that is what you did to escape the hands of the Caucasian Masters during slavery; you pointed your finger at the next Black guy for your failure in finishing whatever job it was to finish, and the other Black guy got whipped or burned to the stake or hanged or genitals cut off or wife taken away and raped. You did that.

Recognize the "cup of love" and put to practice your spiritual disciplines daily. Look inside yourself! Stop calling your Black women bitches and whores. Truthfully, Black women have always stood by their Black men before, during, and after slavery. Some Black women's attitudes changed when they noticed the Black man's desire for the Caucasian woman. That same woman who lied to them and got them hung, beaten, and put in jail. But who did the Black man run to after being beaten down? They came to the Black woman who would oil their scars and wrap them in a bandage of love. I was once one of those Black women with an attitude. So, I wrote harsh words to the Black man, and it went something like this:

Don't Diss Me

(An Excerpt from a *Disrespected Black Woman*)

"You Black men dare to diss me! After the slave masters whipped you, you not only needed my empathy but my warm breast to rest upon." Don't Diss Me!

"You Black men dare to diss me! After losing your job, you needed my ear to listen to your whining, and after giving you my ear, I gave you my money until you got back on your feet." Don't Diss Me!

"You Black men dare to diss me! After Christ died and you hid behind closed doors in fear for your lives, I tried to tell you that He rose again, but you called me crazy. He gave me the command to carry His resurrection message. If you don't believe me read Matthew, Mark, Luke, and John." Don't Diss Me!

"You Black men dare to diss me! You called me senile and crazy because I'm rejoicing in Christ when He met me at Jacob's well. I thought you cared about me." Don't Diss Me!

"You Black men dare to diss me! We carried you for nine months and nurtured you until you could develop into the patriarchal monster you are today. So, if I'm senile and crazy, you are the product of this senile and crazy African American woman." Don't Diss Me!

"You Black men dare to diss me! You hid behind my educated mind when it came to talking to the insurance agent, the broker, the realtor, the banker, the childcare director, the marriage counselor, the guidance counselor, and the judge. Remember, you wanted me to be silent." Don't Diss Me!

"My fellow Black men, lend me your ears! I will not be silent! My Creator says to speak boldly and make it plain so that even you can understand (Habakkuk 2:2-3). My Creator says that I am more than a conqueror (Romans 8:37) and that I am to be steadfast, unmovable, always

abounding in the works of the Lord! (1 Corinthians 15:58) So, you see, you don't have to diss me because we are one of the same bodies in Christ, who is the vine, and we are the branches. Christ is the body; you and I are the extremities. Christ is the Church in which we enter; black with sin to come out of the church white as snow.

So, remember, if you diss me, you are dissing yourself. Don't Diss me!"
(Written Sept. 1, 2006, at 9:00 am at Glencliff High School after reading the book, *Not Without a Struggle*, by Bishop Vashti Murphy McKenzie).

Go on and laugh, readers. I know it's not quite a poem per se, but it's truth speaking, loudly. We can stop the attitudes and recognize what we have inside, a "cup of love." Another good read for my Black brothers and sisters is Bertice Berry's novel, "Redemption Song," It talks about Black people returning to the joy once shared with each other; page 134 reads:

"She looked to Miss Cozy. You mentioned earlier about the movements of the twenties and the sixties. You were right. Real progress was made. People were just learning to tell our own stories and love ourselves. Something always came in and snatched it away."

Ross agreed. "He added that every time Blacks had gained a little ground, though, their movements had been destroyed by government infiltrators and webs of deception."

"You're right about the government," Miss Cozy agreed, "but we played a part in our own downfall." "How is that?" Fina asked.

"Ross is right, they harassed any Black person who worked for change. Even writers and singers were on the FBI hit list. 'The Powers That Be' go to any lengths to stop us from progressing."

"True that!" Miss Cozy added, crossing her arms, imitating a homeboy. "But the truth is, as the Bible put it, 'without a vision, people perish.' Our problem, though, is that we have turned our back on God's vision for our lives and have taken on someone else's vision. Just think about it. Even our idea of beauty is not our own (p. 134-135), *Redemption Song*, Bertice Berry 2000. Ballantine Press. Canada Limited, Toronto)."

Now, to my other racial-ethnic groups. I need not let you know of the hate you have shown to Black people. You do this only to please your oppressors, Caucasians, as if they care more about you. They hate you as they hate us Blacks, only God knows their reason for hating Blacks. They don't know, that a "cup of love" will help them to find out the reason why they hate at all. Caucasians hate other ethnic races too; it's just less noticeable. I can discuss why you hate me, why I hate you all day long, but I rather stick to talking about how we can mend this barrier of racial foolishness through loving one another through the "cup of love" that holds our answers to a better future.

The author of Ephesians has the same meaning to its audience now as it did back then, and that is we are in a spiritual warfare, not a physical one. The inspired Scripture reads, "Finally, be strong in the Lord and in the power of His might. Put on the whole armor of God that you may be able to stand against the wiles of the devil. For we do not wrestle against flesh and blood, but against principalities, against powers, against the rulers of the darkness of this age, against spiritual hosts of wickedness in the heavenly places. Therefore, take up the whole armor of God that you may be able to withstand in the evil day, and having done all, to stand" (6:10-13, KJV).

We must not allow the word "hate" to pass from our lips!

We Can Change Through Practices of Spiritual Discipline

After centuries of fighting each other, we know the consequences of hating. So, let's finish the mission of love that Jesus Christ left for us along with the Holy Spirit and continue to spread that authentic, original love of God that was shown on the cross of redemption. The only way this can be done is to start loving yourself so that you can love someone else. How? Through daily spiritual practices of self-discipline.

These are just a few spiritual disciplines to work on your inner self for a chance to love, and some needed biblical Scriptures to chew on from the *Spiritual Discipline Handbook*, Calhoune, 2005.

CONTEMPLATIVE PRAYER – To develop an open, restful receptivity to the Trinity that enables me to always be with God just as I am.

Definition – Contemplative prayer is a receptive posture of openness toward God. It is a way of waiting with a heart awake to God's presence and his Word. This kind of prayer intentionally trusts and rests in the presence of the Holy Spirit deep in our own spirit.

Scripture – "Meanwhile, the moment we get tired in the waiting, God's Spirit is right alongside helping us along. If we don't know how or what to pray, it doesn't matter. He does our praying in and for us, making prayer out of our wordless sighs, our aching groans. He knows us far better than we know ourselves, knows our pregnant condition, and keeps us present before God." (Romans 8:26-27, The Message). "Now the Lord is the Spirit, and where the Spirit of the Lord is, there is freedom. And we, who with unveiled faces all reflect the Lord's glory, are being transformed into his likeness with ever-increasing glory, which comes from the Lord, who is the Spirit" (2 Corinthians 3:17-18). "This mystery has been kept in the dark for a long time, but now it's out in the open…Christ is in you; therefore, you can look forward to sharing in God's glory" (Colossians 1:26-27 The Message).

Practice Includes – Practicing the presence of God

- Allowing a portion of Scripture to sink deep into the heart as a prayer to God.
- Practicing breath prayer, simple prayer, prayer of the heart
- Practicing centering prayer
- Resting in God and allowing the Spirit to nudge, fill or speak
- Wasting time with God
- **God-Given Fruit** – developing prayer that depends on trust more than giving God information about what he should do
- Living in the awareness of God's presence within me
- Move out of "doing" prayer into "being" prayer
- Learning to let go of distractions in prayer

- Letting God love me

DEVOTIONAL READING – to prayerfully encounter and surrender to the living God through attending to Scripture.

Definition – Devotional reading or hearing of Scripture requires an open, reflective, listening posture alert to the voice of God. This type of reading is aimed more at growing a relationship with God than gathering information about God.

Scripture – "Turn my heart toward your statutes… Oh, how I love your law! I meditate on it all day long… How sweet are your words to my taste, sweeter than honey to my mouth!... Your statutes are my heritage forever; they are the joy of my heart" (Psalm 119:36, 97, 103,111).

"For the word of God is living and active. Sharper than any double-edged sword, it penetrates even to dividing soul and spirit, joints, and marrow; it judges the thoughts and attitudes of the heart. Nothing in all creation is hidden from God's sight" (Hebrew 4:12-13). "The word is very near you; it is in your mouth and your heart so you may obey it" (Deuteronomy 30:14).

Practice Includes – prayerfully dwelling on a passage of Scripture.

- Listening deeply to God's personal word to you
- Reading not to master the text but be mastered by it
- Staying with one text until the Lord prompts movement to another
- Reading for depth, not breadth
- Contemplative and formational reading of Scripture or other devotional texts.

God-Given Fruit – keeping company with Jesus whether he speaks to you

- Seeking and listening for a personal word from God
- Dwelling in a text until it begins to live in and master you

- Responding to God's Word with your heart and spirit, not just your rational, cognitive, and intellectual prowess
- Softening of your heart so that the head-heart schism is mended and you live more and more out of love
- Having Scripture guide your dialogue with God
- A growing receptivity and submission to God's Word

DISCIPLING – To be in a relationship where I am encouraged or where I encourage another to become an apprentice of Jesus.

Definition – Discipling is the process of equipping, training, and encouraging another in his or her apprenticeship to Jesus. It means journeying with and helping another to grow in knowledge as well as in the virtues and character of Christ.

Scripture – "So then, brothers, stand firm and hold to the teachings we passed on to you, whether by word of mouth or by letter" (2 Thessalonians 2:15). "Make it your ambition to lead a quiet life, to mind your own business, and to work with your hands, just as we told you, so that your daily life may win the respect of outsiders and so that you will not be dependent on anybody" (1 Thessalonians 4:11). "Go out and train everyone you meet, far and near, in this way of life, marking them by baptism in the threefold name: Father, Son, and Holy Spirit" (Matthew 28:19, The Message). "I no longer call you servants because a servant does not know his master's business. Instead, I have called you friends, for everything I learned from my Father I have made known to you" (John 15:15).

Practice Includes – meeting with one another to study the Bible, pray and encourage his or her spiritual growth.

- Teaching and equipping another so he or she can also teach others
- Instructing and modeling Christian virtues and disciplines

- Attending to the worship, faith and obedience of a younger believer by a more seasoned saint
- Intentionally investing in the life of an apprentice to Christ

God-Given Fruit – keeping company with Jesus as you fulfill his command to go and make disciples.

- Becoming a model of service, faith, obedience, and worship of Christ
- Becoming a trainer, equipper, and encourager of others
- Using your gifts for the sake of the kingdom
- Obediently following Jesus in making disciples
- Investing in what lasts – the growth and fruitfulness of others
- Passing on what you have been given
- Becoming a lifelong learner and a lifelong lover

FIXED-HOUR OF PRAYER – to stop my work and pray throughout the day.

Definition – Fixed-hour prayers call for regular and consistent patterns of attending to God throughout the day.

Scripture – "One-day Peter and John were going up to the temple at the time of prayer – at three in the afternoon" (Acts 3:1). "Seven times a day I praise you" (Psalm 119:164). "About noon the following day… Peter went up on the roof to pray" (Acts 10:9).

Practice Includes – Interrupting work at set times for prayer.

- Following the prayers in the Liturgy of the Hours
- Following a personal liturgy for prayer at set hours of the day
- Stopping at the top of every hour for prayer

God-Given Fruit – keeping company with Jesus throughout the hours of the day

- Turning the heart and mind to God at specific hours of the day and night

- Growing detached from the all-absorbing compulsiveness of work
- Integrating being and doing in your daily life
- Developing the ability to hear a word from God during daily activities
- Joining the timeless prayer rhythms of the church throughout the ages

JUSTICE – to love others by seeking their good, protection, gain, and fair treatment

Definition – Justice seeks to help others by correcting and redressing wrongs. It treats others fairly and shows no favoritism.

Scripture – "Seek good, not evil, that you may live… Hate evil, love good; maintain justice in the courts" (Amos 5:14-15).

"But let justice roll on like a river, righteousness like a never-failing stream" (Amos 5:4)!

"Remember those in prison as if you were their fellow prisoners, and those who are mistreated as if you yourselves were suffering" (Hebrew 13:3).

Don't let public opinion influence how you live out our glorious, Christ-originated faith" (James 1:27 – 2:1 The Message).

"Complete the Royal Rule of the Scriptures: "Love others as you love yourself." But if you play up to these so-called important people, you go against the Rule and stand convicted by it" (James 2:8-9 The Message).

Practice Includes – Being responsible to God and others.

- Being a good steward of what you own
- Supporting just causes with time, action, and financial support
- Treating others impartially and fair
- Providing for the poor, needy, and oppressed through the means available to you

- Volunteering for prison ministry, food-bank work, and ministries that serve needs in the local community
- Refusing to buy products from companies that take advantage of the poor

God-Given Fruit – Keeping company with Jesus, living out his concern for the poor and oppressed

- Living sacrificially to bring justice and freedom to others
- Having concern and praying for the oppressed
- Being able to see others through Jesus' eyes of love
- Being other centered rather than self-centered

MENTORING – To accompany and encourage others to grow to their God-given potential

Definition – Mentoring is a relational experience in which one person empowers another by sharing his or her life, experience, and God-given resources. A mentor nurtures an apprentice's personal development, faith and skill.

Scripture – "But Barnabas took him and brought him to the apostles. He told them how Saul on his journey had seen the Lord and that the Lord had spoken to him" (Acts 9:27).

"Timothy, my son, I give you this instruction in keeping with the prophecies once made about you, so that by following them you may fight the good fight, holding on to faith and a good conscience" (Timothy 1:18).

"Likewise teach the older women to be reverent in the way they live…Then they can train the younger women to love their husbands and children, to be self-controlled and pure" (Titus 2:3-5).

Practice Includes – Guidance, encouragement, and modeling given by a more mature believer to a younger one

- Training that equips another to better use their gifts
- Building authentic relationships that provide support, encouragement, and help in specific areas

- Providing or receiving influence, instruction, training, and perspective

    God-Given Fruit – Learning from example

- Practicing teachability and humility
- Building others up in Christ
- Opening my calling, vocation, gifting, and limits to a mentor's wise attention
- Garnering the wisdom of those who have walked with God for many years
- Developing and encouraging new leaders and disciples
- Seeing others grow and change

PRACTICING THE PRESENCE – to develop a continual openness and awareness of Christ's presence living in me.

Definition – Practicing the presence is an invitation to see and experience every moment as a gift of God. It is to live alive to union with the Trinity.

Scripture – "Your new life, which is your real life – even though invisible to spectators – is with Christ in God. He is your life. When Christ (your real life, remember) shows up again on this earth, you'll show up, too – the real you, the glorious you. Meanwhile, be content with obscurity, like Christ" (Colossians 3:3-4 The Message). "The word is very near you; it is in your mouth and in your heart so you may obey it" (Deuteronomy 30:14). "You have your heads in your Bibles constantly because you think you'll find eternal life there. But you miss the forest for the trees. These Scriptures are all about Me! And here I am, standing right before you, and you aren't willing to receive from me the life you say you want" (John 5:39-40 The Message)

Practice Includes – developing a rhythm of living that brings God to mind throughout the day

- Intentionally recollecting yourself before God as you engage in the activities and duties of life
- Seeking to see others through the eyes of God

- Stopping throughout the day to listen to God
- Carrying or placing symbols in your office and home that remind you of Christ's presence
- Using breath prayer, centering prayer

God-Given Fruit – keeping company with Jesus all day long

- Having a deeper union with Christ
- Living a new way of being by letting go of your need to manipulate, compete and control
- Living as though his present moment has no competition
- Receiving each moment as sacred
- Abiding in Christ so that you see him in those who drain, irritate, and anger
- Seeing yourself through God's eyes rather than the eyes of others
- Finding Christ as your joy, sorrow, emptiness, and fullness

- Remaining open and teachable at all moments
- Growing in awareness of your constant need of God

RETREAT – To make space in my life for God alone.

Definition – Retreats are specific and regular times apart for quietly listening to God and delighting in his company. Retreats remove us from the daily battle into times of refreshing, retooling, renewing, and unwinding.

Scripture – "Then, because so many people were coming and going that they did not even have a chance to eat, he said to them, "Come with me by yourselves to a quiet place and get some rest" (Mark 6:31). Be still, and know that I am God" (Psalm 46:10). "Be silent before the Sovereign LORD, for the day of the LORD is near" (Zephaniah 1:7). "He makes me lie down in green pastures, he leads me beside quiet waters, and he restores my soul" (Psalm 23:2-3).

Practice Includes – Spending short times apart as well as extended times away with God

- Detaching from productivity and doing in order to be in the presence of God and attend to his voice alone
- Having longer retreats of two to forty days
- Spending one day a month at a retreat site for time with God
- Having seasonal retreats for rest and renewal
- Withdrawing from life in order to see where your soul is in danger, to seek God's help in reengaging in the battle

God-Given Fruit – in the company of Jesus, being able to quiet the noise inside and out

- Making space in your hectic schedule for the Lover of your soul
- Developing the ability to hear the still, small voice of God
- Freedom from the need to be seen and to produce

- Resting in God
- Gaining perspective on God's work and ways in your soul
- Ability to be, not just do

SELF-CARE – to value myself as my heavenly Father values me.

Definition – Self-care honors God through nurturing and protecting the body, mind, and spirit with their limits and desires.

Scripture – "I thank you, High God–you're breathtaking! Body and soul, I am marvelously made! I worship in adoration – what a creation" (Psalm 139:14 The Message)! "You realize, don't you, that you are the temple of God, and God himself is present in you" (1 Corinthians 3:16 The Message)? "So, love the Lord God with all your passion and prayer and intelligence and energy." And… "Love others as well as you love yourself." There is no other commandment that ranks with these" (Mark 12:30-31, The Message).

Practice Includes – living in a way that honors your body as a living temple for God's presence

- Exercising and eating sensibly
- Observing appropriate boundaries
- Resting and keeping the Sabbath
- Giving and receiving love
- Thanking God for the way he has designed you
- Encouraging rather than neglecting yourself
- Recognizing and practicing my spiritual gifts
- Choosing healthy rather than unhealthy relationships

God-given Fruit – Valuing yourself as Jesus values you

- Having a sane and proper view of yourself
- Practicing self-awareness rather than self-absorption
- Freedom from the "Messiah trap" and trying to save the world to the detriment of your health
- Living within limits without burnout

- Having a deep awareness of God's love for you
- Freedom from addictions that destroy your health and relationships
- Being comfortable in your own skin (Spiritual Disciplines Handbook, 2005).

The Reason We Love: We Are on a "Love" Mission

Historically, we have been given a mission through God to be a blessing to our brothers and sisters who are oppressed. Strangers, they may be, but they are God's loved creatures. Some cultures, including our Americans, do not think it important to care for the oppressed, but God does; His love is beyond all political reasoning. With God's love and blessings, we can be a light in someone else's life.

It is important not only to reflect on mission itself but also to look at other themes in theological mission that shape our understanding of mission. Our understanding and practices of mission will be fundamentally shaped by foundational theological commitments. For example, our understanding of the gospel of Christ, of salvation, of the Holy Spirit, of the church, of sin, of humanity, of the nature and interpretation of Scripture, and more will form our views of mission at a deep level, usually unconsciously.[1] Mission is first of all the work of God; it's God's mission. The church participates in God's mission and therefore is missional by its very nature.[2]

God's Theological Foundation in Mission

God is the foundation of missions, for it is God's mission. We can ask, how is it God's biblical theology of mission? Divine Scripture is God speaking, and in Genesis 1:3, God said, "Let there be light," and there was light" (NRSV). In Scripture, God created heaven and earth and all therein. It is said that Moses, under divine inspiration, wrote the Pentateuch. The Pentateuch holds stories of future redemption for mankind. And, so God said, "Let us make humankind in our image, according to our likeness; and let them have dominion over the fish of the sea, and over the birds of the air, and over the cattle, and over the wild animals of the earth, and over every

---

[1] Michael W. Goheen, Introducing Christian Mission Today (Downers Grove, Illinois: IVP Academic Press, 2014), 86.
[2] Ibid. p. 82.

creeping thing that creeps up on the earth" (Gen. 1:26). God, so supreme, showed his love for humankind before he created them, by having all the resources mankind would need, and after mankind was created, he loved them so much he blew his own spiritual breath inside man, so that God himself will forever be with mankind, until the end of the earth.

A Love So Great

God loved mankind so, that he did not want them to learn of the tree of knowledge of good and evil. Why? Because God foresaw the damage Satan would cause because of good. God foresaw that he would have to save man from evil with love. Scripture says, God spoke to mankind and said, "But of the tree of the knowledge of good and evil you shall not eat, for the day that you eat of it you shall die" (Gen. 2:17). As time passed, the fruit was eaten. And they died, not a physical death, but a spiritual death. They were no longer innocent beings, not ashamed of their nakedness. For Scripture says, "And the man and his wife were both naked and were not ashamed" (Gen 2:25). Therefore, now the flesh was tarnished with the blackness of sin, and none was prouder than the serpent (Satan himself), who introduced the words "like God" to the woman, who then wanted to be like God. The woman, wanting to share her new-found intelligence, gave to her husband, and he ate. Although they had done an unforgiving thing at the time, God did not vanish them from the earth; the very thing he gave them leadership over, no, he showed his love and mercy.

God still loved them so, He only placed them outside the Garden of Eden, never to return. Scripture says, "To the woman, I will greatly increase your pangs in childbearing; in pain, you shall bring forth children, yet your desire shall be for your husband, and he shall rule over you." And, to the man, God said, "Because you have listened to the voice of your wife and have eaten of the tree about which I commanded you, 'You shall not eat of it', cursed is the ground because of you; By the sweat of your face, you shall eat bread until you return to the ground, for out of it you were taken; you are dust, and to dust you shall return" (Gen. 3:16-17, 19). When Adam and Eve multiplied, some of their offspring were evil (for the ground was cursed).

God's Forgiving Nature

As time passed, God witnessed brother killing brother, Sons of God taking wives for themselves (6:2), and evil was spreading rapidly. "The Lord was sorry He made human on the earth, and it grieved Him to His heart (6:16). God still loved mankind and wanted His mission of redemption to be fulfilled, so "Noah found favor in the sight of the Lord" (Gen. 6:8). But then the people became so wicked that He destroyed all, except Noah and his family. Here is another place in time when

God could have destroyed everything, but the love He had toward mankind would not allow it to happen. Nevertheless, God took a special nation of people to Himself, through Noah's bloodline [Israelites], and made a covenant with Noah. Scripture reads, "Then God said to Noah and to his sons with him, "As for me, I am establishing my covenant with you and your descendants after you, and with every living creature that is with you, the birds, the domestic animals, and every animal of the earth with you, as many as came out of the ark" (Gen. 9:8-10). Noah and his sons multiplied the earth as God requested, but evil was not far away. After Noah passed away, the people all got together and wanted to make a name for themselves by building a city and tower toward heaven. God said, "Come let us go down, and confuse their language there so that they will not understand one another's speech" (11:7). I believe this started the different cultures in the world today.

Abraham Chosen

Initially, God would find another to work His mission of redemption through. God did not want to fail or see his people destroyed. And, through this mission God used an Israelite by the name of Abram (later Abraham), to be God's blessing and God's purpose through Israel to bless the nations. God's blessings upon Abram, however, are not intended to end in Abram. God ultimately desire's that these blessings upon Abram overflow to bless the rest of humanity through him.[3]

Abraham was a man of good faith and dignity who was also tested by God, like we all are today. God asked him to sacrifice his only son (22:1-2), and he did all that God asked. Abraham was so faithful and loved by God,

---

[3] Terry Briley, The Foundation of God's Mission and Humanity's Place In It: The Story of Israel (Nashville, TN: Zondervan Press, 2011), p. 43.

that God allowed a ram to be found in a bush for Abraham's sacrifice. Another attribute to Abraham was that he showed hospitality and love to strangers (angels unaware to him), a progression of God's mission. Genesis 18: 1-5, 8 announces that:

> "1 The Lord appeared to Abraham by the oaks Mamre, as he sat at the Entrance of his tent in the heat of the day. 2 He looked up and saw three men standing near him. When he saw them, he ran from the tent entrance to meet them and bowed down to the ground. 3 He said, "My Lord, if I find favor with you; do not pass by your servant, 4 Let a little water be sought, and wash your feet, and rest yourselves under the tree. 5 Let me bring a little bread, that you may refresh yourselves, and after that You may pass on – since you have come to your servant." 8 Then he took curds and milk and the calf that he had

prepared, and set it before them; and he stood by them under the tree while they ate" (NRSV).

God has a variety of missions, within missions, and succumbing to strangers is just one of many missions He will work through His people. God's mission goes beyond feeding strangers and helping the oppressed. God blesses in love, mercy, grace, forgiveness, inspiration, deliverance, and compassion, qualitatively [there is none to compare with him], quantitatively [he is beyond measure]. Protective, yes, He is the only God who can give salvation, sanctification, and glorification; He helps in depressed situations, growing pains, disobedience, hopelessness, and loneliness. All these traits intertwine in God's mission of love "to go" and bless one another. Abraham was a blessing to his people. From the foundation of the world, God has worked his mission of blessings not through Abraham only but through his sons, patriarchs, who became the fathers of many nations.

God took Abraham from Ur and said to Abraham "Go from your country and your kindred and your father's house to the land that I will show you. I will make of you a great nation, and I will bless you, and make your name great so that you will be a blessing" (Gen. 12: 2-3). And, so, this "going out" starts a mission of blessings, and the making of nations and promises only God can make for His people until the one comes who will fulfill God's purpose and plan for his people Israel. "God's promises are made in his infinite wisdom as part of his eternal plan and are backed by his matchless power."[4] Now, as Scripture speaks, through Abraham, Isaac, and Jacob, Israel must have faith in God, their Creator, that he will keep his

---

[4] Scott J. Hafemann, The God of Promise and the Life of Faith (Wheaton, Illinois: Crossway Press, 2001), p. 94.

promise until it is fulfilled by, Love. "In Israel, however, history is the arena of God's activity. The focus is on what God has done, is doing, and is yet to do according to his declared intention."[5]

When God's people became disobedient, time after time, He would send prophets, inspired prophets of God to warn them that he will not allow their arrogance to hinder his purpose of salvation to all. God worked yet another mission through Moses, who delivered God's people out of slavery into a land promised from the beginning of his covenant with Abraham. He said, "To your offspring I will give this land" (Gen. 12:7). Canaan was his promise to them.

The prophets prophesied of a coming Messiah who will fulfill God's purpose. Isaiah announced, "How beautiful upon the mountains are the feet of him who

---

[5] David J. Bosch, "Transforming Mission": Society of Missiology Series, No 16, 15-56 (2011): p. 17.

brings good news, who proclaims peace, who brings glad tidings of good things, who proclaims salvation, who says to Zion, "Your God reigns" (NKJV)! The message of Isaiah is that Yahweh has not abandoned his promises.[6] God allowed them to see two parts of his three-part mission [multiple offspring and Canaan]. The ultimate blessing will come through an incarnate God, 100 percent human yet, 100 percent divine. As we move further into God's theological mission of love and salvation for his people, we will see that "A new David is coming, and there will be a new exodus and a new creation. Yahweh will pour out his Spirit, especially upon his servant, and this servant will bring in the new creation and the new exodus. But he will do so in a most unusual way.[7] God's mission, our mission, will not fail…

---

[6] Thomas R. Schreiner, The King in His Beauty: A Biblical Theology of the Old and New Testaments (Grand Rapids, MI: Baker Publishing, 2013), p. 348.
[7] Ibid, 348.

As God's redemptive story continues through Moses as a deliverer of God's people, there will be another who will come to reconcile us all back into God's love that is tried by Adam's fall, or the fall of mankind. There will be another, prophesized by prophets of old; a priest, a prophet, a king, a Messiah, since these names are befitting, one name supersedes them all "love," Jesus Christ. Through God came an incarnate love to bear our sins upon a crucified cross and to set us free to "live" sinless (sin is now a choice). Love is truth and honest and beautiful. God's whole missional story of redemption is based on love. The spirit that God blew into mankind that lies within us is love. So then, how is it that we sometimes mistake love for lust, an imitation, and a false pretense type of love that blind-sides us when we are not participants of God's missional story?

When the real love died on the cross, was buried, and resurrected by His Father on the third day, Jesus told us that salvation reigns! And the story lives on through the Holy Spirit within us. "Behold, I send the Promise of my Father upon you; but wait in the city of Jerusalem until you are endued with power from on high" (Luke 24:49, NKJV). "We are the mouthpiece, we are the horn blowers, we are the contextualization of missional love through the Holy Spirit until the end of days" (J. L. Seay).

A Circumference of Love / Church Mission / Community Mission / School Mission (Protecting our Children from Immorality)

What kind of people are we? What kind of person is your postman? "The question hardly seems to matter at a function level. Whoever delivers mail to your address has a job to do, and the point is to make sure that the job gets done, not to worry about the morals of the person who does it.

In fact, the man may have been cheating on his wife the night before, but so long as you get the mail the next morning, so long as the message gets delivered to you, that doesn't matter (to you)"[8]

Does it matter that our children are surrounded daily by people and teachers like "the mailman," as long as the job gets done? And so, we get our children to public school on time and to their various sporting events; we must ask, in what ways is their character being trained? Could it be that we are "giving away" the moral education of our children to the forces of American society and leaving their Christian education behind as an afterthought?[9] What happened? When and why did the church leave out of the public system in which our children's very lives depend on knowing

---

[8] Christopher J. H. Wright, Biblical Theology for Life: The Mission of God's People (Grand Rapids, Michigan: Zondervan Press, 2010), 29.
[9] David E. Fitch, The Great Giveaway: Reclaiming the Mission of the Church (Grand Rapids, Michigan: Bakers Books 2007), 202.

Christ as love, true love? Not to say that we, as Evangelicals, don't do the same when we can overlook the need for a living community of Christ to habituate our children into Christ and form their character."[10] Therefore, the church community provides the context of acceptance and forgiveness by God through the cross of Christ, which makes possible the confession of our sins and the removal of repression and denial in the Christian life.

    Yes, the character of our children should matter to the church because they are our present and our future. We have a mission, a biblically legitimate mission, and in its contextual capacity, it includes the children so that they can do their part in the sharing of the gospel. "One of the dangers with a word like "gospel" is that we all love it so much (rightly) and want to share it so

---

[10] Ibid. 203.

passionately (rightly again), that we don't take time to explore its full biblical content."[11]

A love story (God's story) told once at bedtime, has stopped. "Such comprehensively transforming good news cannot be concealed! Indeed, the very nature of the "gospel" is that it is good news that simply must be announced, as we saw from its biblical roots in Isaiah 52:7. The gospel, therefore, must be heard as "word of truth" (Ephesians 1:13; Colossians 1:5, 23), and on being heard, it needs to be received and believed for what it is" (Thessalonian 2:13).[12]

For example, let's take our precious, impoverished girls, our teenagers. If they don't know the story (the whole story of God's love) when approached by one who says, "I love you," and is not truthful, how can they challenge this lust for love pretense? God's love has

---

[11] Christopher J. H. Wright, Biblical Theology for Life: The Mission of God's People (Grand Rapids, Michigan: Zondervan Press, 2010), 31.
[12] Ibid. 193.

been kicked out of the public school system, where they spend much of their time. Have we failed to teach them about the love of Christ? Or that Christ is the ultimate love, here and now, and not just in the Old Testament or New Testament or the Early Church!

We don't do catechesis, the initiation of the child into the language and ways of Christian life and practice. We treat Christian education as another educational piece alongside several others in a whole developmental program for our young. As a result, sixteen years into our children's lives, evangelical parents often find their children oriented to another world, entirely different from the Christian world the adults know and assumed their children were learning."[13]

---

[13] David E. Fitch, The Great Giveaway: Reclaiming the Mission of the Church (Grand Rapids, Michigan: Bakers Books, 2007), 203-04.

As a child growing up in Nashville, Tennessee, in a public school system, I know how it feels to want love, true love from a young man, only to find out it was only lust he was seeking. My parents did not talk about God's true story of love and redemption, I'm thinking, because the speaker really didn't know how to preach the whole story of God's love. You see, we were separated on Sundays from our parents (figuratively), they sent us to a Baptist church on one end of the city, and they went to another Baptist church on the other side of the city.

Eventually, I figured out why? Because it was seven of us and we did not have the church attire my mother wanted us to wear to go to the large church our parents were attending. And our pastor was only preaching fire and brimstone. If you didn't do this or didn't do that, you were going to hell. However, in the school system, we (parents) are surprised when we discover our teenagers are governed more by the secular cultures of media, sports, and capitalism than the ways of Christ."[14]

In my story as a teenager, I believe if I knew the whole story of God's love, I could have taught the young man what I was taught, and his love for me would have been real, truthful, and beautiful. Instead, I was hurt and confused because he got what he wanted, sex, and I did not get what I wanted, which was true love.

Today, parents are still relying on someone else to teach our children how to lead a virtuous life instead of getting the child and the whole family involved as one with the church's mission of God. And, following up on what is going on inside the classroom. "Because, what we say and pass on is not backed by a powerful cultural community of life into which the children are initiated,

---

[14] Ibid. 204.

the secular culture overwhelms our children by the time they are sixteen."[15]

Indeed, today "when we understand virtues in these terms, we see that the public school itself must assume the status of a tradition to teach virtue successfully. In other words, the public school system must give stories that are illustrations of virtues, give purposes behind the virtues, and offer a way of life in which the virtues make sense."[16] Therefore, likewise, training our children in temperance because the focus is necessary to be joined to God's greatest created purposes for sexuality is different from training children to be temperate for economic or physical health."[17] As stated before, the children must continue the spreading of God's redemptive gospel story of Christ through the Holy Spirit to be contenders in this spiritual warfare.

---

[15] Ibid. 205.
[16] Ibid. 211.
[17] Ibid. 212.

The apostle Paul tells us that our "attitude should be the same as that of Christ Jesus" (Phil 2:5), "Let this mind be in you which was also in Christ Jesus." In school and out of school, in church and out of church, we should be imitators of Christ, prepared to help others learn of His ultimate love so they can practice that same love on others when they say, "I love you." Christians [our children] must be prepared to go where Christ would go: to the poor, to the marginalized, to the places of suffering. They must be prepared to die to self to follow Jesus' radical lifestyle of self-giving and sacrifice."[18] There is no age limit on discipleship; remember that Jesus was twelve when he stepped out on his parents to teach and listen to what the leaders in the temple said about God's story.

---

[18] Michael Frost, Exiles: Living Missionally in a Post Christian Culture (Peabody, Massachusetts: Zondervan Press, 2006) 54.

Surely the real mission of God's people is to get out there and spread the Word, witness, evangelize, tell people about Jesus, and tell them how to get saved,[19] love is part of being saved. It takes disciples to make disciples, and Jesus had spent three years teaching his disciples what it meant to be one. It involved practical and down-to-earth lessons on life, attitudes, behavior, trust, forgiveness, love, generosity, obedience to Jesus, and countercultural actions toward others.[20]

God's mission story is not over! Through the Holy Spirit, I see children as disciples or witnesses carrying on the gospel of love to fellow classmates, boyfriends, girlfriends, and even the people who never knew the story. However, even those of us who are not called to be evangelists are called to be witnesses to the

---

[19] Christopher J. H. Wright, Biblical Theology for Life: The Mission of God's People (Grand Rapits, Michigan: Zondervan Press, 2010), 163.
[20] Ibid. 163.

Lord Jesus Christ and to be willing to speak up for him when opportunities arise.[21]

Let us stop putting the blame on schools, political economics, parents, or churches; let the children move on.

If we are engaging in the work of new creation, in seeking to bring advanced signs of God's eventual new world into being in the present, in justice and beauty and a million other ways, then at the center of the picture stands the personal call of the gospel of Jesus to every child, woman, and man.[22]

The intention is to prove God's love as the ultimate love [historically and missionally] through Jesus Christ in this present day. Time after time, love is used for lust, and if you don't know where true love really comes from, you will fall in despair and

---

[21] Ibid. 164.
[22] N. T. Wright, Surprised by Hope (New York: Harper Collins Press, 2008), 225.

depression. Knowing Christ is having joy that no one can remove from you.

QUESTIONS FOR PERSONAL REFLECTION

A CUP OF LOVE has been identified in this book as "God's Love." On the basis of racism, what are your personal feelings on loving another's culture?

_____

_____

_____

_____

_____

_____

_____

_____

_____

A CUP OF LOVE has been identified in this book as "Respecting Others Worth." On the basis of forgiveness, what are your personal feelings on forgiving others and forgiving yourself?

_____

_____

_____

_____

_____

_____

_____

_____

_____

_____

_____

_____

A CUP OF LOVE has been identified in this book as "Practicing Spiritual Disciplines." Which of the spiritual disciplines in this book do you use and admire the most?

_____
_____
_____
_____
_____
_____
_____
_____
_____
_____
_____
_____
_____
_____

A CUP OF LOVE has been identified in this book as "Change." What type of changes do you need that would change your life for the better?

_____

_____

_____

_____

_____

_____

_____

_____

_____

_____

_____

_____

_____

NOTES

NOTES

BIBLIOGRAPHY

Anselm K. Min, *The Solidarity of Others In A Divided World: A Postmodern Theology after Postmodernism* (New York, New York: t and t Clark Publication, 2004).

Christopher J. H. Wright, *Biblical Theology for Life: The Mission of God's People* (Grand Rapids, Michigan: Zondervan Press, 2010).

David E. Fitch, *The Great Giveaway: Reclaiming the Mission of the Church* (Grand Rapids, Michigan: Bakers Books 2007).

Michael Frost, *Exiles: Living Missionally in a Post Christian Culture* (Peabody, Massachusetts: Zondervan Press, 2006).

N. T. Wright, *Surprised by Hope* (New York, New York: Harper Collins Press, 2008).

The Reason We Love: We Are on a "Love" Mission

My Three-Part Research Paper on God's Authentic Love Toward Us...

ABOUT THE AUTHOR

Dr. Janet L. Seay-Stanley grew up in Nashville, Tennessee, and now lives in Kentucky. For the last thirteen years, she has been educating herself on the things that she felt were important to her. She has studied early childhood development, human behavior, social-work, spiritual formation, conflict mediation, and Biblical Exposition. She always loved and enjoyed being around people who are positive and enthusiastic about life. Books are her fantasy that takes her away from the madness in the world. Her inspiration is the ordinary conversation about what God has done for others and how she could help others get back on their feet. "It's the unsaid and gaps in conversation that she finds most valuable" (The Tide Between Us). Her most challenging thesis paper was entitled, "Christology: Defending the Deity of Jesus Christ," and she aced it! A Cup of Love is the inspired truth about humans in a good way. Truth will follow us through eternity's end.

www.ingramcontent.com/pod-product-compliance
Lightning Source LLC
Chambersburg PA
CBHW050654160426
43194CB00010B/1940